Man of a Certain Age:
Happy Alcoholic Moves On

I am back. Odds are, if you're reading this, well...you somehow made it through my my first "Man of a Certain Age:" via CreateSpace or Amazon.

I began this one before I even published the first one. Weird? I know.

We have George Clooney to thank for sparking this effort. After the highs and lows of the holidays of 2015, we are all back into our home, school, and work grooves, respectively, and I'm bored again. It was about this time last year that I started hand-writing my half-life memoir that eventually made it into this MacBook Air and was shared with a very few loved ones.

This morning, after my breakfast of mini-croissants and fruit smoothie, I was left to wait for the daily fog (real and metaphorical) to lift and the outside temp to rise above freezing, so I could go enjoy my daily power-walk in comfort. I've vowed to focus more on real stories about real people and to cut out even more television each day, which, fortunately, did not work this morning. After my CBS This Morning fix with Gail, Charlie, and Nora, I moved on to mindless searching and landed on one of the most story-filled shows on tv, The Actors Studio with James Lipton. George Clooney was the guest from this 2012 interview. A 2-hour interview, so it must have promise, and it was just fine for the first hour or so. Other than dashing good looks & rocking salt-and-pepper coif, he is married one of the most beautiful, entertaining, and smart women we each know....I had no idea how much we had in common.

His reaction to questions about his upbringing and where he was from hit me like a bolt out of nowhere. His "insert joke here" or like retort to the questions is just what I would offer, if I were ever honored with such a stage and program. His upbringing was strict, as mine was. He grew up and fled to freedom in ways that I can identify with even today. He had a disdain for authority and for the path everyone took to their version of "success".

And, he took on sales jobs and opportunities that he wasn't always completely proud of...been there, done that. Most of all, at our ages, just a few years apart, neither of us will settle for any project nor opportunity that is not fun and enjoyable with others of like mind, regardless of the pay. He said it. I was reminded of it, through his words. This is why I'm still searching for the next one, caring for our home & family as best I can, and writing my story to entertain and inform love ones and strangers along the way.

Thank you, Mr. George Clooney. You've unknowingly been a great help to me today....and my wife really loves you. I'm sure you get that a lot.

Moving on.

I recently attempted a role in an insignificant spot on an episode of "Snapped: Killer Couples" on the Oxygen Network...I was the nosey neighbor trying to help the detectives figure out what happened. I had a picture of the experience above, but replaced it with my beachy homage. More importantly, the grilled pulpo (octopus), on the first page, was the best...and my collective Camino cures are my year 48 focus...trying new things, enjoying good to great things, and keep walking forward with only those who really matter. And, get back to my new church, along the Camino de Santiago.

If you recall, 2015...especially that wonderful summer...changed me quite a bit. It was a very enlightening year for me. No need to rehash that one, assuming you did your duty and read my first attempt at writing.

In 2016, our girls are grown now and taking on new adventures. Our half-baked little dudes are just that and about to enter hormonal hell. Our mid-life challenges are evolving, challenging, and pretty damn funny too. This Man of a Certain Age will be dealing with those in a bit.

For now, suffice it to say, that this new year brings even more new beginnings, new opportunities, and new characters into our lives that will intrigue, interest, and humor us. Entire new families will be joining our crazy world this year and beyond. Buckle up, campers. We are all in for quite a ride.

At least we're not quite dead yet...

We made it through the 2015 holidays, but the many family conversations still ring in my ears. Our conversations with our kids, younger and older, are always informative and/or entertaining. Those with our older relatives are just what they are...mostly depressing and/or annoying.

We have a proven theory, My Love and I do, that everyone has a mental switch that flips at a certain age. That switch is one that does not really consider the impact of words, thoughts, and opinions on others. That's fine when it's just a kooky point about something random or silly. However, it's something else altogether when it's about the people you love, hardships of those, or just really important challenges and issues. I could pinpoint too many holiday conversations, as we all can, that should have been avoided, but happened anyway. Enough about that. Let's fast-forward to just the other day. It happened again. A sweet lesson about how not to be when old. I love my aging mother. She's a sassy saint to many she knows, which probably numbers in the thousands. She's just my loved widow mom to me, who certainly gave me a chunk of my blunt personality. It's just a shame that she's still Baptist and that we cannot improvise a drinking game every time she visits. If we could, I would do a shot of whatever we have handy every time an illness, MD appt, or death was brought up. At over 80 years of age, it seems that about 90% of one's day is consumed with suffering, attempts at healing, and loss, if our conversations are any indication.

The other 10% seems to be eating and doing other things to distract from the above negativity. Mom was sweet enough to bring her homemade potato soup over, since My Love was not well. But, she had to drop it off and return home to shower for her next funeral, her ninth funeral in just a week. I'm not lying. 9th! In 7 days! How does that happen? I'm just not sure. The last two were 50-something men with heart failure. That will get you thinking. This is the American South where hearts fail like nowhere else.

No one should have to endure such, but I have another theory about this. Once you reach a certain age, widow/widower or not, most people retire from work and, me thinks, also retire from dreams, passions, and life in general. Sure, there are still octogenarian mountain climbers, globe trotters, artists, surfers, and lovers of life...thank God. I plan to keep the fires going. But, the body changes in many ways and reasons and dreams to do things eventually get replaced with reasons and excuses not to do certain things. That's just a reality that I have experienced in my little world over and over.

Funerals, MD appointments, and like gatherings of like people going through similar suffering and loss seems to replace the dreamy gatherings of like people in fun places...at least in this country. In Spain, Costa Rica, and any given island, our conversations never drown in our humanity, but lift up to the moment, the immediate experience, and the engagement of like minds, hearts, and appetites. I may have spent my first half all-American, but, as of last July, I intend to spend my better half of life as if I were from other lands. And, eventually, we will make that our full-time reality and push the flipping of our morbid switches to the very end, if flipped on at all.

That cannot stop the natural course of events and loss that occurs with all of us. But, we can control how we react to changes in our situations and inevitable loss, without those things driving our daily thoughts and conversations.

I'll never get over losing my dad and I think about him a lot, especially every time I look at a mirror. However, I don't talk about him all the time. I need, we all need, to talk about the here and now and the dreamy things to come.

We've been to our share of funerals, but maybe 9 over the last decade, not the last week. Heart-breaking ones with a child dying in her sleep to the expected of older loved ones to a stunner of one of a friend my age who dropped dead while chopping firewood. All very sad and not forgotten.

All offering reminders about the uncertainty of life and that we all need to live for more moments and take nothing of importance for granted. That's what I experienced walking across Spain with minimal provisions and nothing but the comfort of strangers who wished us well and/or provided for us along The Way. Again, that pilgrimage and time with both of our daughters changed me, mostly for the better. I say mostly, since my tolerance of commercialism, consumerism, and pure waste of time and resources is virtually zero now...and I'm surrounded by it everyday in this country of my birth.

My Love asked me what I wanted for Christmas, per usual, last year. My answer was swift and easy. Experiences. That's it. I have given away a lot of my closet and I still have too much. No More Stuff! Probably not what she was expecting. Thus, we have trips planned. Lots of cities, towns, and parts of this country and others that our family has never experienced. Merry Christmas to us. Moreover, I intend to return for what will hopefully be an annual pilgrimage to the Camino de Santiago of Northern Spain, but solo this next time. My next book is calling me there. I need to experience the Camino and her faces of God alone and compare my first two for this book, for my own soul, and for my own base of growing intellect.

It's these experiences and engagement in life that will keep one's perspective real and delay or avoid the "switch flipping" right to the end, of which I hope and pray is decades away. I have too many fun books to write about experiences, people, food, and places to come! At least we're not dead yet, I keep thinking during every conversation with my mom. Her life is here and, Lord willing, will never be mine, at her age. First of all, I plan to keep traveling the world with My Love, like my parents never did. I plan to ask our kids and grandkids about their life experiences and share the same when asked. Most of all, I am going to attempt to stay mentally sharp enough to never, never discuss my inevitable ailments, MD appointments, personal hygiene, and death & dying with them, for as long as possible. If I don't care to hear about such things at my age, just imagine what topics of conversation would do to our Millennial kids, our younger boys without a generational hashtag, and all of their respective kids. Yes, our grandkids are already on my mind. Not the squishy babies that everyone adores and dresses up in ridiculous costumes and gowns. (Don't get me started about baby boys in Christening gowns! Yikes. Like most things at church, it's mostly about presentation, as opposed to enriching one's soul) I'm talking about living, thinking, expressive kids that share our bloodline. Our four kids watch our every move and take our leads or ignore us, at will. What will it be like for those who are two generations removed from the Captain and My Love....not peepaw nor poppy nor whatever here. Just call me Captain or Cappy, if you like. It will be so much easier and sensible when we finally have that perfect catamaran down in the USVI/BVI's someday. Meanwhile, while we wait for marriages and little boogers adding value to our family experiences, we have the here and now with half-baked and grown boogers that make us smile, laugh, frown, and/or tear up on a daily basis.

They are our focus for now. Tacky t-shirts and all...anything goes on our rare beach trips together now!

Sex

Yes. There. I said it.

How do you think those four brilliant kids were created?

The recovering Baptist in me shivers a bit at what's being typed here.

So are, I'm assuming, our grown children who are reading this.

Sex is not what is used to be. Sex was recreation, at will, and the time was almost always right when I was young. Granted, there were only two partners over these formative years and I was married to each young woman...not at the same time...I'm not a Mormon.

Let me be blunt. Making love, which is what committed, life-long partners do, is so different in one's 20's. It's new. It's fresh. It's full of less fat, more muscle, and vastly heightened energy and stamina sans pharmaceutical aides. Arguments may occur from time to time and make-up sex seemed to be a thing, but I don't really recall such...ever. It was always something to do, as opposed to television, other exercise, and eating. That last point seems to not change much with age...but the spontaneity certainly does. This is the part where this dad blames the kids...sort of.

Kids certainly do distract a romantic, "eros" love in a remarkable way. However, kids are a product of such and deserve no blame. They are a gift and men of a certain age know that. Life has trade-offs and sex is traded away for so many other mutual pleasures and greater goods. In other words, sex addicts and/or narcissists should never procreate. It just will not produce healthy, functioning adults down the proverbial road.

Kids add so much wonderful value AND worry & stress to daily life that it's not a good combination for Hollywood-esque romance & living. But, really, what is? That's a fantasy that I do not believe even Brad-jelina enjoy. So many kids, so little time and energy to share with all of them. The former is a given, but the latter is most important.

It is a fact that everyone's own pituitary-based, human-growth hormones begin to decline in their 20's. It eventually bottoms out, barring HGH drugs and supplements (which I helped sell years ago), and you are left in your 40's to figure out a better diet, healthy and frequent exercise, and ways to keep the frame and guts you have in shape that defies your age. Much easier said than done, which I know quite well. However, that's all we have at this age. Drugs to me, except for my damn Lipitor, are not an option. Well...okay...except Cialis too. It is handy. There's even a daily dose for daily fun and ability to pee with greater dexterity.

But, that's not for me. The 36-hour version works well for romantic getaways and holidays and wherever My Love has a little inspiration. And, that little tear-drop pill does the job quite well, when the mood hits us.

Again, truth be told, there's just a lot better things to do with our late 40-something bodies than sex. We care for our kids, more than anything. We sleep almost as much. Never underestimate the power of sleep every night and naps when you can quiet everyone or send them packing for an afternoon. Siestas are a must in Spain and other healthier countries, as they are a must for me almost every day. My Love even takes them in her company car, if some nosey whoever does not tap on the window and ask if all is okay. Nap, people! We cook and clean. We each exercise for several hours per week. And, we catch our favorite 2-3 shows on network tv and binge nightly for a week or two when Netflix dumps "House of Cards" and "Frankie and Grace" on-line.

Oh, we chat too. My God, how we can chat!

We've had our kids. We've had our 20+ years of love, living, travel, and experiences. We hope for much more to come. But, Marvin Gaye's "Let's Get it On.." is not going to be a part of it. We just need to embrace that.

There are just many better things to do <u>right now</u>, as opposed to sneaking around for a few to a few more minutes of sensual pleasure. Sure, it connects us in a unique way. One that only we two share and have for decades, in a variety of places. Never in two side-by-side claw-foot bathtubs overlooking a cliff...but wonderful indoor destinations, nonetheless.

Lesson for living here: You just have to find your respective passions and that works out well when you have a decade or two past your youth at a certain age. The flames may not be roaring anymore, but they do indeed constantly burn in a variety of "philia" & "agape" loving ways.

Food

One thing that beats sex, hands down for now, is delicious, simple food.

You can just enjoy it for a longer period of time every day and I, personally, rank 30 minutes to 3 hours of pleasure of any kind above minutes of any other. That's just me. I love to cook everyday, which lasts for an hour to several, based on how many meals and just what I'm creating that day. I'm about to get up in a few and whip up a spicy chicken salad dish for me and My Love, so we can fuel up for our marathon basketball Saturday with our two boys.

I love food, if you can't tell. But, it hasn't loved me much in the past. I was raised by a great cook, my mother. She fried almost everything and veggies were overcooked to limp. Casseroles were made and enjoyed. Spaghetti with a meat sauce was exotic, due to that mysterious "bay leaf" that could kill you, if eaten, so my mom would say while fishing each leaf out. Who knew? Needless to say, I had to leave home to discover what a variety of meat, veg, and carb options were out there. Over time, my love of simple food from all corners of the world grew exponentially, as did my cooking abilities and my waistline. I went from a 34 waste, before my practice marriage, to size 44 when fat and happy over a decade or so later.

Then, the ringer went off in my head and I changed things up.

First of all, I knew I was in trouble when going to the bathroom and trying take care of that business became very difficult to reach and finish. Let your imagination run with that one. That was a huge red flag for me. I could still see my toes when standing, but I could not accept difficulty reaching places to do what one needs to do in a hygienic sense.

So, instead of hitting the gym, trail, or any kind of exercise regimen, I did what any spoiled American with too much cash would do. I went and had my fat sucked out of pockets of my torso and waistline. It hurt. It was expensive. It was a complete secret too. I recovered in our bonus suite and our kids were none the wiser. Dad was just under the weather.

It worked for a while, but you would not know it today. Such a waste.

Enjoying the right food, rarely indulging in the bad, tasty options, and burning said food would be the real answers that I needed. So, I walked more, reduced portion sizes, ate mostly what I cooked with healthier ingredients, and did absolutely nothing to reduce my booze intake. It was all about the food and amount of exercise.

I had a joke for years that simple went like "my people don't run, we swagger, we stroll, but, we don't run". Funny to me and my loved ones, but I turned on that joke and it's meaning. I did start to run, in spite of my disdain for all who do such, who never look like they are enjoying it, and frequently requiring knee or other surgeries to repair what they have chosen to damage. Surgery just seemed to be accepted as a given by my like-aged runners. And, when my right knee started popping at-will when flexed in a lying position, it got my attention. So, I asked around and found that it's "just your ACL" and it may go at anytime. Really? Just my ACL? I'm no orthopedic MD nor anything close, but I know that I don't like that hunch, guess, or off-the-cuff observation. My brief running days were over quickly. I had lost weight and that was good, but I did plateau low around 250lbs for this 6'3" frame and I just did not see a svelte me in my future, running or not. I just saw knee surgery, recovery, and titanium implants.

Those are not for me, so I went back to walking and my love of food.

Fortunately, one can love great food, eat well, and still remain quite healthy in middle-age and beyond, but one does have to almost give up one's fried food roots, if applicable.

My latest culinary revolution came in the form of a bullet. My Love shot me. Yes, she pulled the trigger at Bed, Bath, and Beyond and surprised me with a Nutri-bullet Ninja. I was now a culinary Ninja, thanks to her. Never would I just sit and each a variety of fruits each morning, every morning. However, now, I create a fresh fruit/lite yogurt/double-dark chocolate almond Silk smoothie every morning of the week. It replaces my morning coffee, since I gave up that last caffeine addiction to, due to heart palpitation issues over the last year or so. And, the smoothie tastes great. Moreover, it does that regularity thing no one ever wants to discuss. Instead of waiting for "my coffee to kick in", so to speak, the dark, rich, fibrous smoothie gets the job done nicely. I'm as regular and solid as a Metamucil addict, but with no grit. Just seeds. Little seeds from the frozen blueberries (acting as ice) and fresh strawberries, which insists that I brush and floss every morning too. It's a win-win-win. Add some yogurt, along with the almond milk/Hagan-Daz like Silk and we have a winning combo. Fruit, antioxidants, fiber, and a filling glass of what's good for you and can help choke down my Lipitor horse-pill too. With my genetic cholesterol count over 300 last month, I'm out to prove something to my MD. Either the drug is useless and I'm just destined to clog up and die too early. Or, the drug works and I need to keep it, my diet, and vigorous walking going. We shall see and I will report my results in a later chapter. And, again, I digress.

Past that early morning smoothie, I don't indulge in fatty, meaty breakfasts often. Just a tasty English muffin or croissant with olive oil or real butter, depending on what we have, and that's it. I've never been huge breakfast person, vacation travel and special holiday eating not included.

However, like almost every aspect of my life, Spain has changed my outlook on eating for pleasure and sustenance forever. My daughter really enjoyed her cafe' con leche' and simple toast (large half-loaf of fresh bread) with jelly. I, on the other hand, stuck to my no-cafe'/caffeine regimen and chose fresh oj and maybe a croissant with soft butter wherever we stopped for breakfast. If no croissant, I just stuck with my oj. I don't like hard bread. They did a marvelous thing with orange juice. Most stops had this huge contraption behind their counter that would take fresh oranges and dump the right number into the hopper with a push of a button. Then, the machine sliced each, squeezed them intensely, and out poured the freshest juice possible into a rather small, by American standards, glass. A normal juice glass, by European standards...and I loved it. I now know what liquid gold must taste like. Spain is known for their oranges and it shows. They know pastry too and we did enjoy an occasional tortilla (egg and potato quiche-like pie) and hand-held pies too. It was a rare, but tasty treat when a fresh one presented itself. Overall, my point is this. One just does not need much in food and calories to get the day and metabolism going. A few hundred calories will just do. A mix of carbs, fat, and maybe protein (egg and/or meat) will do. Protein can also wait until lunch or snacking.

It just seems much healthier to me now.

Most of all, a small starter, bigger lunch at mid-day, and smaller dinner with no late snacking seems to be the lesson here for me. In Spain, I would save my appetite, as I walked for hours, until we arrived at our intended Camino village or town and we relished a big lunch of salad, bread, wine or beer, and maybe something special...grilled pulpo (octopus) being my favorite and all too rare, except in Galicia, Spain. Salads with tuna, tomatoes, onion, and simple vinaigrettes were the norm and were very tasty. All of this lighter and healthy food was balanced with liters of vino tinto (red wine) and cervesas (beer), based on the town and our euro budget.

I was also very pleased to find fresh markets that sold fresh bread, cheese, fruit, and vino that we could make our own culinary fun every afternoon. Not that we did so with food, but we certainly could. My favorite lazy afternoon was after descending the mountains and arriving in the town of Molineseca, where we found a downtown, riverside hang-out to swim, picnic, and really soak up the Spanish attitude, culture, sun, and sights. Our picnic spread there was the best of my life. My daughter was there. So were two of our new friends from the Camino. We ate, drank, enjoyed our surroundings, and loved a lazy afternoon like I've never done before...it was picnic heaven. Moreover, the tightwad in me was pleased. I found delicious food and wine for 4 for less than 20 euros, which included regional wines for 2-3 euros per liter. Life there is simple and cheap. Sure, there are multi-starred restaurants around, but we did not need that. We enjoyed one for a late dinner, but we did not need it. We just needed lots of sleep, several tasty meals, wine and laughs, and lots of rest and recuperation with new friends who enjoyed the Camino as much as we did.

Simple meals. Simple drink. Simple rest and relaxation. Life anew.

Lastly, who am I enjoying the above with? It would be little to no fun if my new world and life were to be experienced all alone. Okay, I do need to nap alone, but, that's it. Eating alone is necessary, based on others schedules. Sleeping alone? Occasionally is fine, but not every night. There's something comforting there.

But, eating with others is fantastic. It is rarely routine and mundane. It can open windows of conversation about hopes, dreams, fears, and plans for the future. That's some of the power of food. In Spain, we ate dinner with complete strangers most of the time and it was quite enlightening for me.

Pilgrim meals were simple, family style affairs and included local ingredients and recipes that certainly nourished us, but also connected all of us to overcome all of the cross-cultural aspects of the meal. Language barriers be damned, pass the "insalata, por favor". Pointing and smiling conquers all at the dinner table.

Sure, we're talking about a 8-10 euro, 3-4 course dinners with unlimited vino tinto…so, there was no leg of lamb, filet mignon, or blackened salmon. And, that was just fine. Simple, tasty, family style meals were just the nutritional canvas and we all were the impromptu painting in-action. The moments of each dinner were real and can never be repeated, much like our meals at home.

Each one is different, like each day is different.

Dinners on the Camino were quite satisfying, due to the tasty food, for sure, but also due the sense of common purpose and inspiration on the Camino.

If we could only duplicate that in our 7-day-a-week, mundane life here...well, that would be special. I imagine that our experience there is just a European given, especially in rural areas, and we could find the same all over Spain, France, Italy, Germany, and other lovely places over there.

That is living.

All of that being said, it's still a valuable lesson for us. Eat well. Eat small (tapas works). Eat often. And wash it all down with local beer or wine, as the meal dictates. That is my best takeaway from our culinary experience in Northern Spain, which is what I've brought home to enjoy. Sure, we still enjoy roasted chicken on weekends and a slow-cooked roast of beef too, but salads, flatbread pizzas, pastas, salmon, and roasted veggies make our menus work...with lots of Tempranillo vino tinto to boot. No fried foods. No burgers and dogs. No fast food, except when on the road and necessary.

Just mostly the food at the perimeter of the fresh market and minimal options, like pasta and cereal, from the processed foods center of the store. It's as close as I can come to frequenting the fresh markets of Europe daily, but it is a healthier trend to continue for the remainder of my days here, until we return to places we love and remain there forever.

Lesson for living here: Enjoy the taste and feel of everything, the food, conversation, and the company, as well. Those are what make a meal much more than just a meal...food brings experiences, thoughts, and great conversations with family, friends, and strangers (friends to be?) alike.

Cheers!

Health

Health is such a loaded word.

I am no doctor and will never be such a professional. Fair warning.

I am just a man who has lived an interesting life and one who hopes to make it even more interesting to come.

I am not young anymore, but I am not too old to do fun, energetic things. I just choose to spend my daily energy wisely. Today, I write, I read, and I listen and enjoy my favorite podcasts. The Camino Podcast is one such podcast. I'm now on episode 10. Look it up on SoundCloud, if you are interested. WTF is another one. PTI for my daily sports fix works too.

Back to health...physical, mental, emotional, and spiritual...sure, you can target other categories, but I will stick with those four...frankly, that's just enough. Sexual was handled up-front, but fits into physical. Intellect will be grouped into the mental column. Eros, Philos, and Agape love must plug into the emotional side. God, Jesus, Budda, Mohammed, etc. are all lumped in and wonderfully set apart in our spiritual side, as well. Thank God, I say...spoiler alert.

One never really considers their health, past what is seen by others or in a mirror, in his or her youth. Youth is about attractiveness, in different ways, but most of all as a magnet for partners and maybe life-long sex and love. That is the focus. Fun sex for a while and then procreational mating when "the one" is found, for a while or forever, if one is lucky.

Our physical health is determined about so few factors: genetics, physical efforts, energy intake, and energy spent.

I'm excluding illegal drugs, promiscuity, cigarettes, and other stupid life choices...of which I've never "enjoyed" and cannot comment nor judge with any expertise.

It's all about genetics, stupid.

I have a curse that I cannot cure. My mom and dad have left me, thanks to their ancestors, with that curse. My doctors seem to think that a generic form of Lipitor will wrangle my curse. We shall see. I refused to take the pills for a year or so and, now, I'm on a quest to prove it's a miracle drug or a failure. That's my only pill, past holiday Cialis, for now and I hope to keep it that way. I'm now around 270lbs in weight with a pretty consistent, big boy frame of 6'3", thanks to my father. He was a towering man to me, as a child, and he shrunk a bit as I headed fast to middle age. I'm guessing that I have the same effect on our two young boys of 9 and 11 now and that will go away in just a few years. Both of them will be tall and at least one will be thick like me, unless he takes his physical health more seriously than I did in my youth.

We inherit so many things from our parents and pass on the same. Past that gunky cholesterol challenge, I have followed my folks in the world of fun & sun skin cancer realities. As a matter of fact, I just had my first two spots frozen off my forehead and my doc cut out a small dot off my lower back for testing. Another first for me! I'm on the cut, freeze, or burn trail that my parents enjoyed regularly in their latter years. More engaging conversation topics to share there. Yikes.

I, on the other hand, am taking action sooner than later. My full-body exam was a first a she was gentle....My Love has never scanned my entire frame, for good reason, but it went just fine. I'm supposed to return annually or thereabouts, just for kicks and to save my life, if I prefer.

That covers this man of a certain age on the outside. As for the inside, I really covered a lot of this in the previous pages. Food is good. Food can be great. It's the timing, taste, and volume that all count the most. Small breakfast with fruits and light carbs seem to work best for me.

I stay away from meat for breakfast. My dark chocolate Silk and fruit smoothies are very filling and some carbs and/or one or two egg omelets give you a nice balance to start my day.

Lunch is a big deal. It should be your biggest meal, in my opinion and experience. Big salad, little protein, some fats, some carbs...go tapas or the like. Do small plates of things you love. You will get a needed boost from the bread, the meat, the cheese, the veggies, and anything you love in small portions. And, don't forget the red wine. Wine with food is a must for digestion and overall health. Sweet tea and soft drinks do nothing for you. Water is the best, but only offers hydration. Red wine offers tremendous health benefits, relaxation, and much better conversations with yourself, or words typed here, and with others.

Yes, I do drink while I write. My words to tend to come easier and I really enjoy the calming affect of my Tempranillo grapes, just like my time in Spain on the Camino. Life is too short to keep your thoughts inside and leave others someday just wondering what life was like, let alone what old dad or granddad (that's Captain to you) thought or experienced. That's where I am and I refuse to leave such behind for my loved ones.

But, I digress...again.

Dinner has been, like many things in our lives, downsized quite a bit. We just don't need the two or three courses, side dishes, and other fattening parts that creates pressure on the cook, a cleaning nightmare, and way too many calories for our family....and especially our middle-age frames.

Meat is now a once or twice entree per week. We may just be heading to meatless weeks someday. Our indigestion and other gassy issues are down. Greens and more ethnic dishes are great for our bodies. Sure, cheese can happily replace meat and black beans offer great protein (and gas) too.

Tortillas and chips from the same offer excellent, lean foundations for what you fill it or top it with. Just not too many. "Everything in moderation" is one of the most annoying and worn out phrases in modern history. But, at dinner, as the day is winding down and the evening cocktails and vino tinto may flow…it's sound advice for us. Just last night saw our boys eat a good dinner as My Love and I snacked on lime-infused avocado slices on bruschetta with black bean and cheese flatbread slices…and red wine. It filled us up. It did the job. It tasted great. And, our family of 4 was able to catch up together over healthy meals all around. The kids' meals were different, of course, but I'm not getting into that…too many early mistakes there on our part and they are not "men of a certain age", which is my focus here.

Lastly, I remember a time in my youth when my mother would fill me and my dad up each night on snacks. Popcorn was popular, but that mysterious orange nacho cheese with flakes of jalapeños poured over tortilla chips were the best…and worst thing I consumed as a young boy. She was always serving us meals or snacks, with no regard for the portion size nor timing of the caloric intake. My dad's jokes about her skimping on snack portions was handed down to me and I ran with it too. Thus, she really loaded us up with mounds of food each evening, just to shut us up and we all laughed every time. It was the 1970's and early 1980's…who knew? Well, we did not know what that did to us and my young metabolism didn't seem to mind much either. Fast forward to this era and we are instilling the limited to no snacking mindset into our little guys.

If it's not in our fridge or pantry, we can't eat it. It's just that simple. Physical well-being....Feel the burn! Yes, I have joked that my people don't run...but, I lied. I run. I jog. I walk. I wog. I get outside and do what my body says.

If I'm dragging, so is my pace. If I'm feeling good, I walk very fast and build up to a wog (walking to jogging pace). If I'm feeling randy with nowhere else to turn, I run. It hurts. I sweat. My heart pounds out the Lipitor juices like mad. However, the sun calls me, like any day on the Camino. I make my own Camino here on this lovely boulevard near our apartment several times a week. Everyone wonders how I can go for up to 15 kilometers over 2-2.5 hours per journey. I wonder how I can get back to 17-30 kilometers over 5-6 hours per journey per day in Spain. Just very different perspectives, I guess.

Exercise, that falls short of painful injury, is always a great thing.

We Americans love to talk that good game and sign up for gym memberships that roughly 80% of members rarely or never use. My choice is very simple. Until we move to that island or village where we feel most at home, I am choosing to use what God and fellow taxpayers have given us... public walking and running paths and greenways of all types. Forget taking the road with cars...go the path of fellow walkers, hikers, runners, and bikers. Nature and taxes have never created a better investment than those trails that are almost free and easy routes to better health for the mind, body, and soul. It may not be the Camino for now, but it will just have to do.

Eat simple...up to Noon each day. Burn that off and more while drinking water all afternoon....and, then have that small dinner with your family or others that prevents late-night snacking...vino tinto for all too!

Cheers, everyone!

Scorekeeping

We all do it.

It's so natural.

God made us this way, for sure. Flawed.

Fortunately, we live, experience and, hopefully, grow up.

The games changes, as do the scores and just what to score or not.

I exercise in a blessed place, on a blessed boulevard, where I'm more likely to walk past a Land Rover, ten or so per hour, an Audi, a Mercedes, and several BMW's than any number of birds and squirrels. This seems to be more of a luxury vehicle habitat with huge, ancient trees, a brown river, and a beautiful road beside it all. There you go. More scorekeeping.

To my credit, I notice such things much more quickly these days. Credit my having it all, wants and needs, and losing most of those material wants years ago. These days, all I can obsess about is how to minimize the material waste, from my closet to my fridge and pantry to my false relationships with things and fake people too. My scorecard became much easier to keep over the last few years and, especially, after my Camino in Spain. I had no idea that life could just be so simple. It requires getting out of the ordinary of this America to really see how the other fulfilled half lives. And, it is void of plenty of stuff...the stuff of scorekeeping to a fault. I drive a BMW, which rolled off the assembly line in Germany before 9/11. Yes, I will probably own this little 323 for two decades or so and I paid cash for it years ago. That's my score there. It get us around. It serves its purpose. I miss my Lincoln Navigator, my navy-blue 1969 Cadillac convertible, and other cool rides...but, not enough to go into debt again.

We've rented condos for years now too. No maintenance to really consider. No taxes and insurance concerns. Simple, but with zero equity too. I understand that. I also understand how to almost kill oneself by building a dream home and then trying to pay for it when times get tough. Just call me an old soul when it comes to accumulating too much stuff. I'm stressing a bit right now, as My Love has a great opportunity to grow with her company and we will need to move all of the stuff we have in several storage locations, let along our current condo. It's just a logistical thing and I will handle it, at the appropriate time. However, it reminds me, again, how silly I was to buy so much stuff back in the day and now we are saddled with it all. I refuse to leave it all for our kids to figure out. We will sell a little, take the rest, and figure this 1st World problem out.

On that note, the hopeful lesson here is simply to not go after all the stuff you want. Go for what stuff you need and then go for all of the experiences and life-long memories that you and your family can handle. That's really living. Beats death, for sure...for now....

Two days ago, on Easter Sunday, one of our finest attorneys (there are really nice gentlemen out there in that profession) and nicest friends dropped dead at the young age of 57. Sure, we worked a lot. He had made partner and bravely left to start his own firm. He had a modest, 2nd floor office in a 2-story building in our little suburb. Most are located in the tall towers of downtown, where he earned his chops. I did a little business with him and he helped us clean up an issue from our personal, financial collapse. He and his lovely wife hosted us at their lake-side cabin for dinner. Their family of grown kids and grandkids to come are ideal. But, he's dead. Not sure why. Heart attack is what we were told. Christ is Risen, as they say, and Brian just goes away...the same day. Yet again, the irony is not lost on me. He was an exceptional servant of our Lord, husband, father, and just a real guy who probably did not keep score. His score was fine with him.

However, dead men tell no tales and I regret not knowing more of his. As I do those others named Bob, Allen, Phillip, Gary, Chuck, and only lovely Kathleen...just a few who I can recall right now...who left way too soon. Sad for us, but just how their loved ones feel at the time and for years and decades after his or her passing. Not a lot of material scorekeeping left there.

Where does that leave me, after all of the above. Well, I just call my doc and he want to discuss my blood test results of this week. Is that cholesterol still over 300 and clogging me up or did the 80mgs daily of Lipitor do its job. We shall see on Friday. A nurse can't just tell me and order a prescription...no, I must sit down with the doctor, for a price. Even good health is really about someone's cash-flow. Remember that little score and keep it settled.

People of all ages die, for sure. Tragic when young to middle-age and less tragic after whatever age you think death is inevitable. One wicked scorecard it is.

I'm left with this scorecard, as I consider it today:

True, daily, lifelong, love and partnership: 1

Brilliant kids, grown and not so, to great adults: 4

Close friends who just make you smile every time: 25

Years of experiences and learning how to be me: 47+

Height and weight: 6'3" and 275 lbs

Total cholesterol: 300+ (unless the Lipitor worked)

Years to keep this journey going: Who the hell really knows?

Faith

If you've read my blog (www.justbecausetwit.wordpress.com) and/or my first effort towards a weird auto-biography, a lot of this chapter will be redundant. But, redundancy can be just fine. It reminds us of things we forgot or sped by while reading.

I am a Christian. Not the one that I grew up to be. My mom tolerates this, after decades of living and watching me grow into a middle-aged man. My upbringing was schizophrenic. Mom and I went to our Baptist church at least three times a week, twice on Sunday and Wednesday night for prayer meetings. That was understood and drilled into me. I was her companion and her son who needed Jesus too. My Dad, a preacher's kid, on the other hand, worked weird shift-work hours and never went to church, even if it was his day off. You see, my father was a preacher's kid that swore off forced religion many years ago. Did he believe? Was he "saved" and going to "heaven"? Two great questions. I have no clue. I just know that my mother was and is full of remarkable faith and my dad's body is in the ground decaying while his spirit may just be somewhere else...I hope so. I hope it's all true and not just feel-good stuff that we teach our kids and use to get by in such a frustrating to cruel world.

I haven't chosen to attend church, sans funerals, Easter & Christmas, for years now. We are Methodists, a pretty laid back lot of pilgrims and worshippers. As I explained to our oldest girl's friends over breakfast this week, I gave up the ritual of church mornings years ago because I was sick of the small talk, the lip service ("let me know if I can ever do anything for you"), and the pomp and circumstance of dressing up in fancy clothes so you show the most respect for God and his congregation. I'm pretty sure that God listens to the poor guy in a ditch just as much as any one in Brooks Brothers or Vera Wang duds.

On that note, in one of my big purges, I gave away all of my Brook Brothers, Ralph Lauren, etc. to the big boy section of our PTA donation bin... nice clothes for high-school kids who need them to interview for jobs, colleges, etc. How cathartic was that for me? Very cathartic. The lady at the PTA center still asks my mother about when her son may be donating more someday, since she took them to the donation center one time.

Organized religion, and the big budgets propping them up, gives me great pause. More like a great stop. I just stopped cold-turkey. It was not difficult. It was surprisingly easy to drop a Sunday morning habit of over four decades. No one called to convince me otherwise. Pretty darn telling of those preachers and "friends" who truly believe in the ritual. Or...maybe very telling about how others perceive my stubbornness and determination to do my own thing. I like to think that the latter is true and that the former is just a sad result of faux relationships. I just needed to take my limited energy and thought and pour that into the who, what, when, and where of life that matter most to me. I just did not and do not have the time nor energy to pour into faux relationships, hollow rituals, and grandiose places that do not speak to me at all anymore.

Then, as God or fate or my daughter or all of the above would have it, my Camino pilgrimage happened. I found my new church. A church full of beautiful vistas, historic places, like-minded people, helpful Spaniards, and even a disciple of Christ himself, Saint James. Not that we met. He did die almost two millennia ago, but his likeness and maybe his spirit is still there today. It's certainly there on The Way of the Camino in her people and places you engage over your days to weeks of walking, climbing, descending, and absorbing along your way through Northern Spain. I had never been to Europe and my first trip was a 300km+ walk over two weeks, plus commuting time and rest in Madrid. As you may recall, my oldest daughter graduated with her Masters degree and this is the trip she wanted.

Her 23 year-old, healthy body and my almost 47 year-old, stout frame were about to take on something neither of us saw coming.

I cannot nor will I attempt to discuss my daughter's faith. I can only write about the Camino and her affect upon me.

It was a simple renewal of spirit.

I had lost faith in organized religion. My faith in our city and state is at an all-time low as well. America isn't my favorite place these days either. Put all of that together and you have quite a cocktail of motivation to find that much better place for you and those you love.

My faith returned to me in an unusual way on the Camino de Santiago of Northern Spain.

I looked past the rare commercialism of bigger towns and we soaked up the culture and flavors of the smaller villages and towns that truly appreciated the fact that we stopped there, we made efforts to engage in Spanish there, and that we contributed to the livelihood of those who choose to live, work, and play along The Way. For the most part, they are beautiful and engaging people without a fast-food stop, Starbucks, big box store, or any other western trappings anywhere in sight. They eat, sleep, and breathe local food, culture, and vino everyday. It's my new religion.

God loves his sinners. Thus, he must love me. And, he must love it when we discover new people and places of his creation…and our new selves, in that process, as well.   God watched me grow up squeaky clean. He watched me lust after several girls and get absolutely nowhere with them. He protected me from three other girls lusting after me as I ran like the wind from such frightening advances. He watched as I fell in deep love and married way too young. Then, He watched as I became a father of two sweet girls and then an ex-husband to their mother. He watched at I met my one true, romantic Love less than a year later and led us through many a joy, trial, and tribulation over the last two decades.   He watched and/or participated in all of those experiences, including our path to Spain and our brief weeks on our first pilgrimage in Europe. Much more to come there.

God is up there somewhere, I'm convinced. This world is too smart and certainly unique within our realm of telescopic sight and understanding. It's just awfully special and cannot be here as a result of a cosmic chance. There's a reason for our world that no one will ever figure out. That's God's job, if He so chooses. Otherwise, we take our faith and run with it…or walk fast with it, in my case. Walk on. Walk daily, weather permitting. Walk the trails and greenways often. Most of all, get back to the Camino and walk your pilgrimage as often as time and money allow. Walk on The Way with St. James, his pilgrims, our Lord, and your thoughts, cares, & worries.

Human Vices

Well, how loaded is that heading for this chapter?

We all have our good and our bad. Here's a Man of a Certain Age's bad side, of which he's has in control or fails miserably to control. Only those around me know the difference.

Smoking

Tried it in college, away from my folks. My Dad could have retired very wealthy from Phillip-Morris with his first sales job in the 1950's...but, he quit early. Too much traveling. Sweet wheels and all. He was the man... the man with cartons of carcinogenic love for the masses of Appalachia. He gave it up, as he did smoking. My Marlboro Man attempt was short-lived too. I would draw that white cylinder outside our freshman dorm...but I never inhaled. The fucker choked me. Is that what smoking is all about? Choking??? Really??? If I couldn't gag it down, why was that smoke even supposed to be there? After a few packs of faux smoking, my intellect took over. Swisher sweets, I bid you farewell, as well. Life moved on.

And, very few things make me as melancholy as beautiful, young women outside smoking like there's no tomorrow. I see them around downtowns. I see them outside the sandwich shops. I see them on the Camino de Santiago. Like me, I did not see the repercussions of gluttony and enjoying food and drink to excess. In them, there's no difference. Immediate pleasure in exchange for a lifetime of trying to prolong what you have unwittingly tried to destroy. Smoke, fat, too many carbs, and other pollution...there's no difference. But, you can choose your diet. Nicotine and other drugs are another thing.

I pray to God that our grown kids and little guys never get hooked on such a drug. Vino tinto and the like, sure. Dad can always use a beloved drinking buddy. Nothing wrong with that!

Prejudice

Everyone judges everyone.

That is a fact.

It's in our DNA.

Dogs do it, in regards to character, me thinks.

Most animals do not. They just see what the being before them can gain them...much like Wall Street executives and career politicians.

I on the other hand, keep most of my prejudices to myself. Now, My Love knows most of them. It's what we do. She is smart, savvy, and drop down gorgeous to me. I cannot hide any prejudice from her, let alone any given emotion. She's just that good.

I covered my racial prejudice that was passed on to me in my first "Man of a Certain Age" volume" It wasn't pretty, but it was honest. Growing up the the southern parts of America makes open-mindedness really hard. Bigotry, homophobia, and other sad realities are just they way they are. I'm convinced that our brains are etched with those thoughts and feelings that can never be purged past childhood. And, it makes me sad.

Many of our world's problems are spawned by such and I just don't think, at my certain age, that we can do anything productive to change it. We just have to adapt and tolerate.

I never jumped into the theatre like I should have, because it was a gay thing to do. I liked girls. I could never be an artist, because I'm not a gay guy. How fucked up was that? Enough said.

Thank God that I was the first of my immediate family to attend and graduate college. My first getaway from our small community led me to a small college with a mix of characters. Suddenly, my prejudices were smacked in the face by guys and gals of all colors, ethnicities, and even sexual preferences. It was shocking and, actually, refreshing. Sure, I hung out with our hetero pals, for the most part, but the world certainly opened up a bit for this guy, in spite of myself.

In short, God created us all. We have no clue about exactly what He thinks now or way back in time. He just gave us our gut and intellect. Are you New Testament or Old Testament folk? That should tell your tale. I'm am a New, but I land mostly in the area that no one really knows any absolute truth. Therefore, we should just stick to being the best we can be and let the chips fall where they may. That's just me. I block out sad people who think they know the one true way to anything. I open up to those who will listen and maybe alter their thinking a bit to a lot based on new information. That is totally contrary to how I was raised. Totally.

Social Media

I'm sure that God does not concern himself with such, like radio, telephones, television, and the internet. As for us, we most certainly do concern ourselves with such. Selfies! Dear God....I have made them too, but do you have to have a long stick to maximize your literal exposure...or GoPro's! Really. At my age, it is certainly beyond me.

My oldest girl's selfie stick broke on our first day on the Camino de Santiago...and I was pleased. I never said so. She had sunk a whopping $10 into it at her local grocery store...lesson learned.

Granted, I took a ton of pics and a few videos on our pilgrimage through Spain. Nothing wrong with that. I posted to my blog when free wifi was available too. We used FaceTime to connect with our loves back home. Social media has so many positive attributes and ability to connect with family, real friends, and far too many faux friends. It's that last group that's so disconcerting. However, I use social media, at my age, as a photo album, a journal, a communication tool, and as a medium of record for my kids and grandkids to learn about that old guy they knew, wish they had known better, or never knew...I'm a little long-range thinker that way.

Kids should use Instagram the same way and not as a tool for self-esteem and self-worth, based on likes and timing of such. Deleting pics when likes don't come in as fast or as furious as one likes...really? Not a problem for men of my age. We just post and move on.

Twitter is a waste of time and you miss most of it, if not online all day long. I just let that auto-post feature do all of my tweets for my via FB.

All other platforms seem to be replacements for real exchanges, real conversations, and real relationships that don't just "disappear" in a predetermined number of minutes. I need simplicity and most social media platforms do not deliver simplicity nor the breadth of what I want to share.

Facebook is king to me for the fact that it is free and it has an endless capacity for a variety of life's lessons, memories, experiences, and love and hate...with a handy blocking feature. You would not believe how many blocks I've clicked on local boobs who have nothing to contribute there and to society as well. I'm sure that I have been blocked, as well.

That's the beauty of it all. Accept those who enrich you and your mind...block those who dump hate, prejudice, or just ignorance on a frequent basis. And, most of all, Facebook does calculate your preferences and ranks your feed accordingly, which is the greatest gift of social media. Love your customized FB feed!

Tattoos

I don't get them. Maybe, back in the Polynesian way...maybe.

Today? Plunge ink into your skin for art and/or message sake?

I don't get it. I never will. Enough said.

Swearing

I do get this. I do it. I enjoy it, when provoked. I use versions of the f-word, as often as needed. So many variations exist. So much relief comes from mumbling one under my breath or just saying in for all to hear, when no one is around. One of my favorite podcasts is named WTF. Go figure. Most of my favorite podcasts are on NPR, where WTF will never be...but it's a guilty pleasure, nonetheless.

I'm not going to detail my profanity here. Let your imagination run wild with that one. I'm just saying that a man of a certain age, who has lived through the divisive melancholy 1970's, the heroic and divisive 1980's, the recession and recovery of the 1990's, and the terror and financial collapse of the 2000's, comes out of such with a new appreciation for "fucker", "fuck off", "fuck you", and just "FUCK!!!" Just saying.

Adultery

Like smoking and tattoos, I just don't get it. It's what men of a certain age seem to do. It's amazing how many are willing to screw around and how many women think that grass is greener. I just don't get it. It's a crushing blow to families and relationships for a lifetime and beyond. Ick.

Ignorance

Ignorance is, indeed, bliss…most of the time….assuming that you don't want to educate those you love and others who may be able to pass on concepts, thoughts, and, God forbid, wisdom to others and future generations.

Personally, I love some of my ignorance. When others ask me about my opinion on local politics, the latest, local newspaper headline, or anything asinine about our backward little town, state, or our region of America, I'm happy to plead ignorance. I've learned that activism means little to nothing if you aren't in the various "clubs" or social circles of such club members. And, if most to all are fairly self-serving, what's the point?

I like the Wall Street Journal and the New York Times. Both offer a global perspective on life from left and right. Both cover the bigger world, like no cable news channel can. Both still employ very smart reporters and columnists to detail the things that matter the most around the globe. That's where this man of a certain age should be.

Inform yourself. Enjoy yourself. Fight the ignorance that comes from living, playing, talking, and staying in your little, tiny town, suburb, and community. Get away. Go global. Travel out of your particular bubble and you will enjoy a much wider scope of perspective.

You will truly see how not the other-half, but the other 96% of the world really live.

Truly, I have no interest in experiencing every spot on the globe. My education over the years has taught me that tropical locales of the Caribbean, villages and town of Western Europe, and a few other spots around Europe, and parts of South America, are my remaining experiences. That's all that I need. Hopefully, My Love will agree and so will our kids and grandkids.

Politics = Business

So boring.

I'm no political pundit.

I'm no business tycoon.

I'm just a guy who's been deeply involved with both for years.

The equation above holds true. You cannot separate politics from business and vice versa. Getting elected is all about who you know and who they know to get you there. Getting ahead in business is about being at the right place at the right time with the right crowd to fund you, as well.

They are, essentially, the same thing and overlap, as time passes, everyday, in small town America...which is most of this country. Anyone of a right mind cannot help growing very tired of that. I certainly did.

After years of activism for social programs and then more years of supporting those who talked a great game, my better intuitions caught up with me and told me that I was wasting a great deal of my time here in our little backward town. That same small group of families and their minions controlled most of the activity and supposed "progress" moving forward, which better resembled place-holders and status-quo stooges in local, elected offices. Keep the golden goose happy and don't rock any boats, it seemed and still seems today. My Love and I cannot name one single elected official locally, regionally, or the state house or Governor's mansion who is inspiring. In short, we are done.

Same for our national representatives...no Hope & Change left there.

My last vote for president was in 2008. I know this. If that "hope and change" vote fell on deaf and dumb ears then, how the fuck will any vote truly matter eight, twelve, sixteen, etc. years later?...especially with the liars and boobs of the 2016 campaigning for leader of the free world.

Am I going to ever participate the electoral process again? Probably not. Our states are pretty fixed as Red or Blue and only a few have any real electoral sway for the top job. If we end up in Florida, for part of the sailing season, who knows? As for now, the field of "leaders" is so weak or mismatched that I cannot imagine voting again anytime soon. Only God could change my mind, at this point. Really.

Drugs

I'm all for the legal ones. They get me by. They pay our bills. They help us save for our future life. Drugs are very good, if used for specific ailments and to drive realities away like... the plague?

Illegal drugs, on the other hand, are not things that I'm familiar with from way back to modern life. I know what weed smells like, since I took that in outside of the bathroom in high school and around our lefty leaning neighborhood of the 1990's. It has a very distinct aroma.

Coke, crack, LSD, heroin, and many others never crossed my path as a young nor old man. It just wasn't something I attracted nor pursued.

Booze, on the other hand, has always been my entertaining to abusive friend. I do love to imbibe. Privately, at parties, at the homes of those who share my taste for liquid love…they are all fine by me….to a point.

Workaholism

It is all-American. Practically Japanese. Work. Work. Work.

I watched my dad do just that, out of necessity.

I watched my bosses do just that, out of greed and control.

I watched so many think that work, or looking like work, is success.

Lord knows that I have seen, heard, and felt the sting of workaholics.

I always wanted far more.

And, more is just what I worked not so hard for, thanks to the above.

I have always said that "freedom" was my greatest paycheck.

Even as I deposited six-figure profit-sharing every 3 months…freedom.

Our girls knew and know their dad very well, in spite of a divorce.

Our family was free to travel and explore our country, in spite of her.

I took on challenges and jobs, based on the ability to go, as needed.

Others around me felt that their loyalty to any business pays off.

It may, every two weeks, but loyalty and longevity is not business.

Business is about "what have you done for me lately?", for sure.

That's why working yourself to the end is no great ending at all.

Just do what you need to do and build into what you want to do.

General Assholery

Steve Jobs.

Ideal entrepreneur. Visionary. Self-made billionaire. And.

One huge asshole.

When did it become acceptable to ditch those who helped you create magnificent solutions to everyday challenges, to ignore the child you helped create, and to pretend that the parents you have don't exist...even when you were adopted by another loving couple. His dad served him breakfast at a diner and he never acknowledged him.

His daughter begged for his attention and she received very little, after he refused to acknowledge his fatherhood. He challenged, threatened, and derided almost all in his wake and he is celebrated as one of the most successful businessmen of his era. I see him as a total failure, if character means anything.

I'm sure Edison, Carnegie, Ford, Churchill, Roosevelt, Einstein, and plenty of other game-changers of this modern world have been less than ideal husbands, employers, friends, and maybe even fathers. They just couldn't help it. It's how they achieved their era's great success and how they kept others out of their way and in their respective places. It's how it was done.

As for this era, I cannot stomach disappointing the ones who I love, on a regular basis. Missing appointments. Missing ballgames. Missing school meetings. Missing birthday parties and other silly things. Missing all moments that are fleeting and can never be captured in one's mind, one's camera, one's Facebook album...and one's heart. They are all gone too soon.

That's life. Don't spend it like Steve Jobs, CEO, www.assholery.com.

Yes, you may think of me as such for insulting the dead. Kudos.

Virtues

Benevolence

Giving of oneself to others, kin or otherwise, is one of the best investments one can make in his or her family, friends, and strangers alike. My Love reminds me of this on a regular basis. My mother does too.

I'm more than a bit crusty to the thought of benevolence towards others outside of family and close pals, after giving and giving over the decades and seeing only, in my myopic way, mostly self-serving types determined to keep their jobs and missions primarily benefiting those pulling out a regular paycheck. I could say the same for the "business" of our historic church, which has a multi-million dollar, annual budget and capital campaigns begging tens of millions of $$$'s, as the church elders see fit.

You see, I've served on too many non-profit boards and church committees to be diplomatic and impartial about this. Way too many.

I have consulted, to very little affect. several more non-profits. They are pretty much all the same.   Start strong with great intentions and missions, get comfortable, and keep the status-quo going, regardless of real ROI for those contributing time, talents, and cash.

Boards with most members who are padding his or her resume' or just killing time in his or her not-so-busy schedules make me nauseous.

Executive Directors who are less than qualified, or less than confident , to take on the Board with specific service needs, funding requests, and real justification for those investments are normal.

Unless really, really inspired again, like with politics, I'm out.

At my age, my benevolence is targeted and is invested only where my ROI is guaranteed to be maximized…family and very few close friends. As our four kids all grow up into parents themselves, I will be ready to spread myself as thin or thick as needed in probably four distinct corners of the world to help them and their immediate family with their challenges and celebrate their victories. I am in training for such family marathons with not finish line in sight.

And, I don't feel one bit of guilt about leaving all of the past accomplishments, failures, and related relationships behind, in this training process.

Our family keeps my concerns very simple. I only take calls from those who matter most. I interact with my new, beautiful, global, Camino family everyday on FaceBook. And I take care of our family business and my health needs, along the way, too. I have always needed a simple life and I have that right now...and plan to keep it going until the end.

Focus on what gets you and yours by, on your terms, every day.

Focus on what inspires you everyday and you will be fulfilled.

Men of a Certain Age need to focus, simplify, and stay honest

Middle-age gets better. I promise.

Recovery

Recovery. In any context, the word presumes damage of some sort and the need to get better. I stepped into our sunken den almost a decade ago and my physical therapist friend said, in his best Arkansas accent, "Man, man, once you're about 40, man, you don't bounce back quick". He gave me six months to recover my hamstring from TAKING ONE STEP! He was right.

Another time, around that time, I did who knows what to my forearm. Something strained and guess what? Six months, man. Another six months for the pain to go away.

Jeff was right. Men of a Certain Age take time to heal. I am right there. Those two "injuries" were innocent enough and freakish in their events. I still don't know how I can be so careful not to strain myself…and it still happens.

My knees popping were the latest events that led me to gear down and power walk moving forward, not running. My knee stopped popping and the healing has seemed to occur. Listening to your body will tell you all you need to know.

Most of all, as I revealed in this title and in my first book's title, I know that I love booze. I have since I left my Southern Baptist upbringing. I married, had two sweet daughters, and divorced while drinking along the way, but not to excess…just not to Baptist standards. I move back home and eventually met My Love and we dated with split entrees and carafes of cheap wine or margaritas. I was never a beer guy, in those early days. Too gassy.

As my business interests took off, we entertained more, we collected wine, we bought a silly SubZero wine fridge to care for our collection…oh, we had one helluva libation room…a butler's pantry, I believe we called it.

Life moved on and so did my tastes and tolerance levels.

No need to cover the boring variety of booze, but you can assume that there wasn't much we did not enjoy. Martinis, bold red wines, and lemon-peel infused vodkas kept flowing from home to home over the decades.

I grew a tremendous tolerance to any drink that did offer a lot of fun at parties, at home, and around town. However, as with most vices, that road needed to come to an end.

If you read my first book and/or my blog, you know how my effort to detox myself came about. It was in the cards. Too many signs. Too many people to love and appreciate. Our family is growing fast, as well. Something had to give and I did.

Past my breaking point last fall, I even had a sign from my personal doctor, who asked about my drinking habits. I told him, when asked to quantify, "too much, every day". He offered meds to help and I told him that that was not necessary…but, just him suggesting that made me think.

I went back to my Camino summer and winded down my tastes and tolerance levels to something far more European. Vino tinto (Spanish red wine) now takes the lead with my tapas lunch and evening insalatas and meals. Cervesas once or twice a month, with guy talk or sports. And, just a small amount of clear spirits to take the edge off, as needed, as opposed to a daily thing. My Love enjoys vino tinto, as well, fortunately, and we enjoy our little corner of Spain most nights.

Lastly, I have never been professionally diagnosed any drinking problem..but, if it drinks like a duck..well...I know. I took control. I am taking control each day. I still enjoy drinks alone or with friends, but I do it much differently. I'm still a big guy with a great tolerance.

I'm just more focused on the people and conversations happening in the moment. Food and conversations are enjoyed far more when your senses are not dulled and you can still put thoughts into coherent words for others to enjoy. My self-inflicted recovery is up to me each day, each week, and each life event.

Last weekend, when sharing time with our daughter's new family to come, she asked if my glass had water or something else. Another sign. It was just ice water, but she's been trained to know better.

Listen to those signs, as sad as they may be. Now, our wonderful hosts did have a Scotch there that I enjoyed a lot. On the rocks. Hadn't done that in forever. It was another sign. Like junk food in the pantry...if it's not available, you cannot consume it. It will be a few years before we entertain a full bar again for gatherings and parties to come. But, if the Caribbean rum is as cheap as they say...well...we shall see.

Louis Anderson, the comedian, just said, on the radio, that his alcoholic father gave up drinking at the age of 69. Wow. At that age, what's the point? Just kidding. I may get there someday, as well. My body has changed so much from 40 to almost 50 that I can't imagine what I will need to boost or cut out of my life by 70 years of age. Where we are will also dictate such, since I'm too cheap to overpay for any treats that are not indigenous to any region where we live. That goes for fresh food and local beverages alike. Tasty, but cheap, is how my second-half life recovery rolls.

Longevity

Love

Nothing quite makes you want to live a long time quite like love.

Unconditional love is the best. Get it from your dog. You're golden.

Get it from your closest friends. You're golden, too.

Get it from children, babies to all grown up, and you are blessed.

Get it from your partner, the one you took a chance on and she or he with you, and…well…there you go. You have the best chance to be the best you, stay healthy, and live longer…the best chance, but no guarantees.

My Love has been covered quite well in my first "Man of a Certain Age:" book and again here, with lovely photos. She is my one, true love, if you cannot tell.

I've been thinking a lot about our 20-something age of meeting and launching our new life together, since our oldest girl is getting hitched this year to her Love. I keep picturing my daughter and this old dad standing there, at the end of the carpet, and about to make our way down the aisle. Tears? Maybe. Advice? For sure. Short and sweet. And, after two wives and two brilliant children from each of them, I may know what I'm doing when it comes to unconditional love. My few seconds of advice will go something like this.

"My dear, I love you. You are loved. Enjoy this "eros" love, as long as you can. Work on your "philia" love moving forward. And, God willing, be blessed with "agape" love for your best friend and partner as life goes on."

Thanks to Wikipedia, I believe this informs and details where my head was when I first fell in love...and as we found real, long-lasting love...

Eros (/ˈɪrɒs/ or /ˈɛrɒs/; Ancient Greek: ἔρως *érōs* "love" or "desire") is one of the four words in Ancient Greek which can be rendered into English as "love". *Eros* refers to "intimate love" or romantic love. The term *erotic* is derived from *eros*. *Eros* has also been used in philosophy and psychology in a much wider sense, almost as an equivalent to "life energy".

Young love. I wish all young people well with such love. It's sweet.

Then, it should grow even more.

Philia (/ˈfɪljə/ or /ˈfɪliə/; Ancient Greek: φιλία), is one of the ancient Greek words for love. In Aristotle's *Nicomachean Ethics*, philia is usually translated as "friendship" or affection.

Sure, philia can apply to any friendship and any relationship, but, for me, it relates to my best friends, who I can count on one hand...okay, a few fingers.

The best of the best being My Love of over 20 years, as of today, who has loved, laughed, cried, and travelled with me and many others on our journey together...that is our developing philia love past our early eros love that attracted us to one another.

Then, there's this...

Agape (Ancient Greek: ἀγάπη, *agápē*) is "love: the highest form of love, especially brotherly love, charity; the love of God for man and of man for God." Agápē embraces a universal, unconditional love that transcends that and serves regardless of circumstances. Ancient authors have used forms of the word to denote love of a spouse or family, or affection for a particular activity, in contrast to philia (an affection that could denote friendship, brotherhood or generally non-sexual affection) and eros, an affection of a sexual nature.

Christianity developed Agape as the love of God or Christ for humankind. In the New Testament, it refers to the covenant love of God for humans, as well as the human reciprocal love for God; the term necessarily extends to the love of one's fellow man. Although the word did not have a specific religious connotation, it has been used by a variety of contemporary and ancient sources, including biblical authors and Christian authors.

Agape love is just something that I believe comes with time with those who matter most to you. Unconditional love would be a more contemporary phrase to describe such a love. God, as I've been told, loves us with an agape love. So, I believe, we are capable of such too. It is reserved for very few or it could be any other love. Agape says that you are special to me. You are not like any other stranger and friend alike. You, indeed, are special to me and I will love you forever, regardless of events, actions, and circumstances.

In my life, I only have a few people who I love with such agape love. You know who they are, as you've read my books.

Developing you true loves through time and experiences and reaching a level of agape love with those who matter most will keep you alive, kicking, and living well beyond anyone who does not open up to and offer such love.

Life is so much better with unconditional love to accept and to give.

My Love....

Beautiful things

Another, big, subjective thing here that allows you to live longer.

God's creations. My Love.

Sunsets. Sunrises.

Works of visual art.

Music. Especially jazz.

Delicious plates of food. Small, tasty plates.

Children having fun, especially your own.

Peaceful walks, hikes, and other adventures.

Any beach. Anytime.

Meaningful conversations, live and interesting podcasts too.

Martinis. Vino tinto. Cervesas.

The Camino de Santiago of Spain.

Traveling to places much different than home.

Making a home where you never feel the need to travel again.

But, travel you must...

These are my, very personal and beautiful things that keep me going, offer me peace, and give me many reasons to keep pursuing my dreams and passions with those I know and love in that agape sort of way.

Stay numb

Life can be hard sometimes. For me, it can be easy to hard all in the same day. Hopes and fond memories drive one way and flashbacks to mistakes and bad memories, which are natural and rare, drive the other way in any given day. I've chosen my selective degrees of numbness to get me by.

The phrase "happy alcoholic" should be self-explanatory.

My Love and I just had our first conversation the other day about my first book title and this series to come. She had no idea that I was going in such a direction with this series. I didn't either, until I just did it.

Staying numb is just another phrase for coping mechanisms.

Quiet walks can do as much for anyone as any chemical alternative.

On that note, I'm going on one right now. Sunny and 65 outside.

(Pause. Take a walk for yourself)

It's the next day and I'm back.

Where was I? Well. Staying numb in one or more ways insulates you and me from the fears, negativity, and overall downers that life tries to hit you with almost every day.

Notes to and replies from our grown kids numbs me from lesser things. So do real conversations with any of our kids, little dudes to grown ladies. Thoughts, observations, questions, and conversations with our kids are a wonderful drug unto themselves. Always different, always challenging, and always educational…and mostly fun. Gracias, family.

Small portions

Keep it small and simple. What do you like?

Tapas? Sushi? Pasta dishes? Filet Mignon? Lobster rolls? Pulpo?

All very doable. Just do it, in moderation, of course

Do it with the most delicious items on the planet and keep it small.

Not a lot to ask. Our middle-age, human frames only need small.

Really. It's a fact. And, we need less and less as we age, for sure.

I've even begun fasting everyday. Not all day, but just a meal here or there and almost no snacking whatsoever. Late-night Cheez-Its are a problem once or twice a month, but that's it. If it's not in the pantry, I cannot eat it for a snack. We keep healthier snacks around and it does take a lot of will power to avoid snacking at all. On the other hand, if I'm not hungry, I don't eat three meals a day. I may or may not have a blueberry-strawberry-dark chocolate, almond milk smoothie...tastes like a chocolate shake, but is really good for you. If no smoothie, I may have a toasted croissant with butter early... or brunch time bowl of left-overs...soup, pasta, etc....or go without anything until an early lunch of tapas, especially if I'm not exercising. Sliced meat and cheese and maybe crackers are my go-to domestic tapas. Keep it light and preferably with meat. Protein and fat for lunch before Noon. That gives me the energy I need for my long power-walks and/or elliptical machine while our boys literally kick it in their Krav Maga (Israeli self-defense) classes. You need energy to go all day at work or, in my case, the 2-3 hours of cardio effort and other more domestic god tasks and responsibilities.

For more about fasting, the science behind it, and how my logic has been validated, find the New York Times article of March 7th, 2016 (current link @ http://nyti.ms/1U88MZe)written by ANAHAD O'CONNOR..

On that referral note, I'm a huge believer in a more European diet. Love Greek, Italian, and Spanish cuisine . Simple, tasty, and usually very healthy with a glass of vino. And, this Mediterranean diet article just arrived from www.spain.info and here's what these fine folks had to say:

"Enjoy food in a healthy way. This is the first proposal in the Mediterranean diet, which was awarded the UNESCO Intangible Cultural Heritage designation. Based on the consumption of olive oil, vegetables and fresh seasonal products, the Mediterranean diet is an example to follow as far as eating is concerned - as well as being recommended by the doctor, it is extremely tasty. Come and discover it in Spain - it is one of its best-known features.

The Mediterranean diet is based on a balanced and complete diet following principles such as simple preparation and the use of fresh, local products, and if possible, seasonal. In Spain you enjoy it in several ways: taste it in restaurants, discover its products in the markets or at a meal with friends, for example.

A diet made in Spain

The Mediterranean diet is the basis of Spain's food and many of its principles are present in the tastiest Spanish dishes.

For example, olive oil is the main complement in the Mediterranean diet. As well as adding a unique flavour and aromas, it is recommended for its health and heart benefits. Do you know that Spain is one of its main producers? The regions of Andalusia and Catalonia are the best known. In order to taste it, we suggest a salad with an olive oil dressing, or recipes such as gazpacho and salmorejo (cold soup made with tomato and bread).

The Mediterranean diet is essentially based on fruit, vegetables, pulses and dried fruit and nuts. They are bursting with vitamins and fibre, and Spain also stands out because of its produce. Some of the most outstanding fertile agricultural regions are in Navarre, Andalusia, Murcia, Balearic Islands and Region of Valencia. The latter is well-known for its citrus fruits. Other essential fruit includes bananas from the Canary Islands, strawberries from Huelva and Aranjuez (Madrid), Vinalopó grapes, and peaches from Calanda (Aragon), amongst others.

The Mediterranean diet also recommends consuming products derived from cereals, such as rice, as a good source of energy. In this sense, in Spain there are great rice-based recipes, mainly in the Region of Valencia, where the most popular dish is paella.

Other products in the Mediterranean diet are dairy products. The regions in the north of Spain are well known for their milk and dairy products, with traditional desserts, such as cuajada (type of curd cheese) and rice pudding. Cheese also complements dishes very often, and some of them are especially tasty, such as the Manchego (Castile-La Mancha), Burgos (Castile-León), Cabrales (Asturias), Idiazábal (Basque Country), and Majorero (Canary Islands), etc.

Amongst the recommendations in the Mediterranean diet we find a moderate consumption of eggs, and blue fish and seafood at least once or twice a week. First, why not try the tasty Spanish omelette?

Regarding fish, Spain is washed by the Mediterranean Sea, the Atlantic Ocean and the Cantabrian Sea, so you can taste many types. Some of the most typical are anchovies (very common in Cantabria), cod (typical of the Basque Country), and "pescaíto frito" (fried fish) in Andalusia, and especially, seafood from Galicia.

Lastly, remember that drinking wine moderately, as part of the Mediterranean diet, is a very healthy habit. In Spain you can practice this with any of its tasty wines. One of the most internationally prestigious ones is Rioja, although there are many more to try.

Things to remember:

The Mediterranean diet is much more than a healthy gastronomic recommendation. It is a way of life that involves preparing food traditionally and enjoying it with friends and family, in a calm and relaxed environment. This is why it has been awarded the UNESCO Intangible Cultural Heritage designation.

You can discover many other Spanish products in the Mediterranean diet and learn about them in our section on Spain's food.

If you would like to taste the most delicious wines and enjoy many activities related to our produce, we recommend visiting our section on the Wine Routes in Spain.

In order to learn more about the Mediterranean diet, you can visit the Mediterranean Diet Foundation's website."

Lots of salads, olive and grape seed oils, light meats, avocados, and Med veggies are key to our middle-age health, along with red wines. Tempranillo and the like Spanish grapes are our current choice. Sure, we enjoy thin-crust pizzas and other baked or roasted treats from time to time. And, during vacations and holidays, we certainly stray from the normal and that's just fine. I cannot imagine going to Costa Rica, any Gulf coast beach, New Orleans, or anywhere cooks and chefs really know what to do... and not indulge a bit. But, I can feel it. Gus's World Famous Fried Chicken in downtown Memphis is the best, but I will feel it all day and maybe the next day. Just keeping it real here. Indulge in your degree of gluttony every once and a while and you will better appreciate great food and being void of indigestion and bloating. I can handle a little gluttony once or twice a month, but no more. Spinach queso is another weakness.

Just move

All of the above, no matter how small the portions, demands that this Man of a Certain Age must move. Just move. Cleaning the house and grounds work, but I prefer to get outside and go. Having just experienced the Camino de Santiago last year, walking is always in my thoughts and plans, as I also plan to get back there solo and with one or more family members who are capable of such a pilgrimage. We have a great neighborhood with a nice river-front boulevard and walking trails. It's not the Camino, but what is a few thousand miles away. Thus, I make it my Camino as often as possible.

I walk. I don't run. I don't jog. I almost jog. Mine is a very fast, long-legged walk that pumps the blood and gives the heart a challenge. Same for an hour on the elliptical machine with a target heart rate of 145 beats per minute.

The sun helps motivate me too. Like Spain, the sun warms one's soul and in many literal ways plus offers vitamin D in no better way.

I try my damnedest to get my 10-15kms in every day via walking our boulevard with Escala, Bond, or any other cool band and/or hitting the elliptical machine with my Pandora or various NPR and WTF podcasts. Yeah, I have pretty diverse tastes. I love instrumental, high-impact music, intelligent conversations, and very honest, sometimes profane conversations alike. There you go.

Whatever it takes to keep me moving. Sitting at home or in the office is every Man of a Certain Age's nemesis. Fat loves for you to sit. Muscle loves for you to move and move often. 3-4 times a week for 2-3 hours. I don't care who you are..at our age...you can find 6-12 hours a week to love, live and prosper longer into old age. Find it. It's in you and you'll love it.

Go for it!

No one...I mean no one...ever told me what I was capable of, as I recall.

I don't blame my parents. No one ever told them, as I recall.

Families can suck that way.

Not ours. We have "broken the cycle", as My Love & I like to say.

Our girls are young adults born in love and raised in twice the love.

Divorce sucks too. But, you can make that lemonade sweet if you try.

Both girls are now grown, on their own, loving life, and with nice guys who we love and who we hope they love & are loved by each for decades to come. Those four all have "gone for it", whatever it is, and we are proud. No matter what you may think about this generation of young people, these four have broken the mold with self-sufficiency, kindness, and brilliance. They go for it every day and we could not be prouder parents/in-laws.

We GenX folks went for it too, but in very different ways. My Love is an uber-accomplished sales professional over 25 years or so. I was as well, over some of that timeline. However, I lost a lot, including my faith in business and organized religion, and retreated to other challenges, like caring for the home-front, our family needs between home and school, and my sanity through journaling and building a few books to tell my tale. My Love is impressed and disturbed at the same time, me thinks. Same for my grown kids someday. We shall see.

My point is this. Just go for it, whatever it may be. You know you better than anyone. No one, even your Love, partner, spouse, kids, nor anyone can tell you what it's like to be you from birth to now. Only you.

If you are a Man of a Certain Age, it's your time to do right by yourself and your family and find that thing, that job, that recreation, that trip, that culinary adventure, that whatever gets your proverbial rocks off and just go for it. Preferably with the ones you love, but maybe just alone.

No one should be able to tell you nor instruct you otherwise.

You have lived your life. No one else. Don't be another's fool.

Live it.

Love it.

Go for it.

Not matter what it is...make it yours and all will be well.

You may not be super rich...but, who cares. It's not all it's cracked up to be. It's actually another burden when everyone wants what you have.

Go for those little and gentle pleasures...hopefully, with those who love you and can enjoy such pleasures with you and yours.

Life is too damn short to succeed and fail alone.

Keep your Faith and keep on keeping on...so to speak...Camino love!

Never, never, never, never retire!

My dad did retire and he, more or less, just wasted away the time and energy to end life with my mom and his family in a big way.

Sure, they travelled a bit. We sent them to Hawaii. The enjoyed the desert of Arizona. We all took beach trips to the Gulf Coast together. However, daily shuffling around the ranch house where I grew up did my dad no favors. He slept, ate, drank huge "guzzlers" of diet soda, and he kept growing bigger to discomfort. He played golf, until he kept getting lost on the way to the course and his truck keys were taken away. Diabetes crept in. Alzheimers took its toll, as well. I'm convinced that a lack of mental stimulation and creativity over many decades and then a lethargic retirement took him too soon, even though 78 is a pretty good run.

He retired. He hung around the house. He died too soon.

My mom, on the other hand, has always looked at rest of any kind as some degree of laziness. She is constantly going past the age of 80. She retired about the time that my dad did, but her constant motion seems to be working well for her. She volunteers at church, at her Baptist food pantry, and other places all week long. She rarely takes a day off, which only happens when she leaves town. Loneliness may have a lot to do with it, but it's mostly her need to be with others ("engagement" says My Love) and be productive. Therein lies our lesson.

Never retire. Embrace something bigger than you. Stay busy with life, family, and travel to new and/or familiar places. New sights, sounds, and conversations can keep you younger than you may feel. I'm convinced of that. It might just be my Lipitor talking, but I feel better in semi-retirement than I have in almost a decade. I plan to keep the semi- going and never really hang it up for good. Too many experiences ahead for all of us.

Dream on!

Dreams do change us.

I dreamed, as a young boy, to be an airline pilot and then an FBI agent....only to get real and conclude that I would have a less-than-ideal family life.....yes, a family was a concern of mine at a very young age. Maybe, my own family drove such concern and desire to do better, be there more, and live a long, healthy life to share with two or more generations.

So, I dreamed smaller. I was my immediate family's first to attend college with a full scholarship, thanks to my personality, not my ACT scores nor my 3.53 GPA over four years of high school. I "dreamed" of a business career. I took the necessary classes, performed well, and transferred on to a big university after getting married. I dreamed about graduating and getting that killer pharmaceutical sales job that my business professors said would be waiting for all of us smart, business types. That dream was a lie.

I had to dream bigger. I took sales jobs that I hated, but had to make the most of. I dreamed of owning my own business and controlling my destiny. That dream came true and fast became a nightmare too. Divorce and lawsuits have a way of crushing such dreams.

I re-invented myself and took another job that I hated. The highlight of that job was meeting My Love at the end of my first week training for that pitiful job. A secondary highlights was my sales partner who was from Iran, who was hilarious, and who opined about how I "sweat beautifully" in the hot summer months. Thank you?

I did dream bigger. I dreamed about finding an entrepreneur who could take my college degree in Entrepreneurial Management, Marketing, and Sociology and mentor me into something no one ever imagined.

Life just had to be better that it had been. Must. Dream. On.

So, I did. When asked about my future role in my first lucrative entrepreneurial gig, I simply offered that I would like to run his company when he, the founder, decides to move on. That was my dream.

It happened. It took some doing, some success, respect, and another caught in one too many lies. Not pretty, but that's business and that's how my dream became reality.

My Love and I were able to travel. We explored our own country like never before. We could afford to look past a paycheck. We travelled consistently to be with our two little girls from my practice marriage. We were living that dream. But, some dreams to end...or, at least, tend to change with age and experience.

I dreamed of a big house with a sunken den and resembling an English Manor. That dream came true too. Then, it went away.

My dreams dialed back to just doing what I want to do and never be forced to drag myself out of bed and interact with others who add nothing to my soul, my mind, and my family's overall well-being. I'm the patriarch, so I'm reminded occasionally, and my spiritual, mental, emotional, and physical well-being is now my daily dream.

I dream about an even healthier, fitter me. I dream about using that healthier frame to play games and hike the Camino and other pilgrimages with my kids, their kids, and strangers alike.

Not regrets about not being a commercial airline pilot, FBI agent, and business guru.

I dream about going places everyday and I thank God for certain Facebook groups (APOC, especially) that bring together lovers of Spain and her Camino de Santiago. (They've now replaced all of my sailing groups, which still offers another dream of our families on our own catamaran during the high-season and no hurricane possibilities. That dream will happen too, if I remain healthy. Sailing is not easy.) Everyday, I am connected with a few people, who I may meet in-person, and 99%+ who I'll never meet past Facebook. It's fine.

I dreamed about a perfect community of like interests and Facebook gives us that. A tremendous majority of my Facebook interaction does deal with the inspiration and practicality of the Camino de Santiago, which will be the focus of my third "Man of a Certain Age:" book. I'm bouncing between this keyboard and my iPhone as Camino forum updates are coming in every few minutes. Today's conversation is around a question about taking a 4-yr old child on her Camino. You can only imagine the opinions in that comment section. I chose Switzerland and stayed down the middle on that. Only a parent can decide for his or her own child. Maybe that child will dream bigger if mom figures out a way to share a spiritual journey with him or her. Maybe not. 4 is awfully young for rugged travel.

My dreams each night are as various as they are vivid. I wake up not believing what just happened. Thus, 24/7, it seems that my mind keeps dreaming and planning today and days to come. Adventures of all types are all there, along with familiar and strange faces that add great flavor to those dreams. I tend to wake up in a better mood. I dream along with others, as I write and read my timeline and plug into the NY Times and New Yorker, as well.

Dreaming big demands going global, which keeps us all dreaming, travelling, and adventuring past this little, southern town. Buen Camino!

Pass it all on!

Why we do what we do every day?

www.ingramcontent.com/pod-product-compliance
Lightning Source LLC
LaVergne TN
LVHW071032070426
835507LV00003B/125